Animal Babies

Photographs

Agfa (11)
Toni Angermayer (1, 40, 46)
AP (36)
Julius Behnke (25, 37)
J. Bokma (32, 33, 43)
Gerhard Dagner (9)
Branibor Debeljkovic (18)
Frese (23)
Georg Gerster (45)
Erika Groth-Schmachtenberger (15)
Robert Häusser (19, 26)
Rudi Herzog (20, 24, 41)
Hans Huber (13)
T.S.lal (10)
Keystone (2)
Genadij Kotin (34)
Jürg Klages (5, 6, 7, 8, 27, 28, 38, 42, 44, 47,
front and back cover)
E. Knöll-Siegrist (29, 39)
Franz Pangerl (22)
Erik Parbst (35)
Hanns Reich (17, 21)
Hans W. Silvester (12, 30/31)
U. Thomas (16)
Lies Wiegman (48)
Walter Wissenbach (3, 4, 14)

Copyright © 1970 by Hanns Reich Verlag,
a division of McGraw-Hill Book Company GmbH, Düsseldorf
All rights reserved
Published in the United States of America by
Hill and Wang, a division of Farrar, Straus and Giroux, Inc.
ISBN 0-8090-2001-7
Library of Congress catalog card number: 73-148232
Published simultaneously in Canada by
Doubleday Canada Ltd., Toronto
English translation © 1971 by Violetta Castillo
Production Office: Rudolf P. Gorbach, Munich
Printed in Germany

Animal Babies

Text: Max Alfred Zoll
Translation: Violetta Castillo

A Terra Magica Children's Book

HILL AND WANG · NEW YORK
A division of Farrar, Straus and Giroux, Inc.

When I was a boy, I did not have a book like this, but I made one for myself by cutting animal pictures from the newspapers and pasting them into a note-book, and for many years that was my favorite book. So I have prepared a new one now for you, to send you on a safari, to India to see baby elephants, to Africa for the small rhinoceros, to the North Pole for the polar bear cub, and to the South American jungles to watch the waterhogs walking with their mother.

Start with the cover where a small dotted leopard cub keeps an alert watch from a hollow for its mother's return. The cub is waiting for the food that the leopardess will bring back from her hunt. The picture on the right shows two young ground hogs. They have just come out of their hole into the meadow.

The black swans come originally from Australia. When it is winter here, it is summer there. This pair, believing spring had arrived, built their nest during autumn. So the cygnets (baby swans) came into a world of rain and snow instead of sunshine.

The young storks have been hatched in a huge nest built on a chimney top high above the streets of the city. There the parent storks feed them until the baby birds can fly from the nest themselves.

The fawn has a spotted white coat which is not only beautiful but also serves to hide him from his enemies. When the doe searches for food, her baby may be left alone for hours in safety among the thicket and shrubs of the forest. Because of his coloring, the fawn blends with the light and shadow of his hiding place.

The roe deer's fawn is alarmed. He is only a few days old but already he looks watchful in the tall grass. He can see and hear well, but his sense of smell is the best of all.

With measured steps in single file, the waterhog babies keep close to their mother. From birth these two can see, run, and swim. The South American waterhogs belong to the rodent family, cousins to the rat and to the mouse, not to the hog as their name would suggest. They are the largest in the family, growing to be over 3 feet long and weighing as much as a hundred pounds. Waterhogs live in the moist areas of the forest, near ponds, rivers, lakes, or swamps. With their webbed paws they can swim very well, both in and under the water. Waterhogs are herbivorous (plant eaters). It is not uncommon to see them chewing grass alongside the cattle in the pasture. Because of this, the South Americans call waterhogs capybara, Master of the Grasslands.

The fox cub peeping out of the hollow was born blind and helpless 10 weeks ago. His eyes opened after 14 days. Another 2 weeks passed before he crept out of the fox hole. He is shy and ready to run into his hollow tree hole when he feels danger is hear.

Both owlets have become accustomed to the protection offered by their mother, the snow owl. They were hatched in a poorly built nest because their parents do not care much for nest building. Snow owls scrape the ground to make a flat trough and that is the nest. Owlets have warm, fluffy feathers and eat rats and birds. When food is hard to find in their northern home, the family flies to the south where it is warmer.

The owlet of the horned owl family still has his childish downy feathers but his wing feathers have already started growing. In a few weeks he will be flying.

Bats are flying mammals. The baby bats cling to their mother's coat after birth. They are nursed and carried even when the mother bat is flying. Even when baby bats are old enough to fly themselves, they love to go for rides holding to their mother's breast.

Shrikes break out of the shell chirping for food. The poor mother bird gets no rest because she has to find worms to feed them from morning till night.

A baby horse is called a foal. It can stand an hour after it is born and is ready to follow the mare (its mother) and the herd. When horses roam the hills, being left behind can mean death for a foal. Wolves constantly circle the herd on the lookout for easy prey, like a foal separated from the mare.

The chamois kids, like most hoofed animals, are ready to run after being born. Very soon after giving birth in a secluded place, the mother chamois rejoins the herd with the kids behind her. The kids are good mountain climbers and can go along with the herd over rocks and stony paths quite easily.

Bunnies are born blind and helpless deep in a burrow. There the mother rabbit cares for them. Bunnies grow fast and within a few weeks they are tumbling about at the burrow's entrance under their mother's eye.

Lambs are often born while the ewes are out grazing. Because the lambs cannot walk and keep up with the flock, the shepherd has thought fully packed them into his donkey's saddlebags.

This mouse tasted the sweet apple and could not stop until it had gnawed through to the core and had turned the fruit into a house.

Cats are usually household pets, but they never forget the need to be alert against danger. This one is purring contentedly in its owner's hands, but it is also keeping a sharp lookout.

The baby donkey is born with long ears. How watchfully and cleverly the mother donkey looks at us! Donkeys are not as dumb as we think they are; they only tend to get stubborn from time to time to suit their own purposes.

One, two, three. One must go on counting to know how many piglets there are in the picture. Sometimes one could find up to 15 or even more.

The kitten is approaching the hedgehog very carefully to inspect his quills.

This butterfly, which is called a peacock's eye, does not know that his flower has been picked, and he continues to flutter his colorful wings.

The hedgehog is not often seen during the day. He is awake and lively only from twilight when he goes searching for food. He eats practically anything: worms, snails, lizards, even snakes, rats, and mice; from time to time he hunts rabbits, raids a partridge's nest and for dessert eats wild berries, mushrooms, and fruits. A surprised hedgehog will try to escape. Unable to do this, he will remain where he is, quiet and ready, rolling himself into an untouchable quill ball with a single movement of his back muscles. A curious scientist once counted his quills and came to 16,000.

The kennel owner has thought this out well so that there will be no more snarling and biting over a bone. Each puppy has his own dish; the mother has the biggest of course.

The whooper cygnet, which is a baby swan, rides on his mother's back as though on a boat. Cygnets can go straight to the water from the moment they hatch. They are excellent swimmers, however when they get tired, they clamber up the swan's back to settle for the rest of the journey in the warmth of the mother's feathers.

The ducklings are at home in the pond, even without their mother.

The young chimney swallow hovers near his mother, pecking time and again inside her opened beak for the food she has stored in her stomach. He will keep doing this until he has his fill. Though capable of getting food for himself, this baby does not mind feeding off his mother.

The brown bear cub would like to climb the tree. But even for someone who is as good a climber as he is, this one is simply too thick.

The baby coati has his mother's snout. Coatis can sniff the insect eggs hidden deep under the bark of rotting logs and with their sharp fore claws scratch them out. The baby learns this trick very quickly by watching his mother do it.

Like all bears, the grizzly can swim well. Cubs, however, must be led to the water by their mother before they lose their fear of getting wet.

Crocodiles, which thrive in warm climates, are sociable animals. They live in the water, in lakes, swamps, or rivers. They love to lie closely packed sunning on the riverbanks. At the slightest hint of danger, these sunning crocodiles can very silently glide back to the water. Crocodiles are hatched from eggs which are almost the size of goose eggs. The mother crocodile picks a well concealed riverbank where she lays and later buries her eggs. The eggs are hatched by the warmth of the sun. The newly hatched crocodiles dig themselves out of the incubating hole. From there on, they are independent.

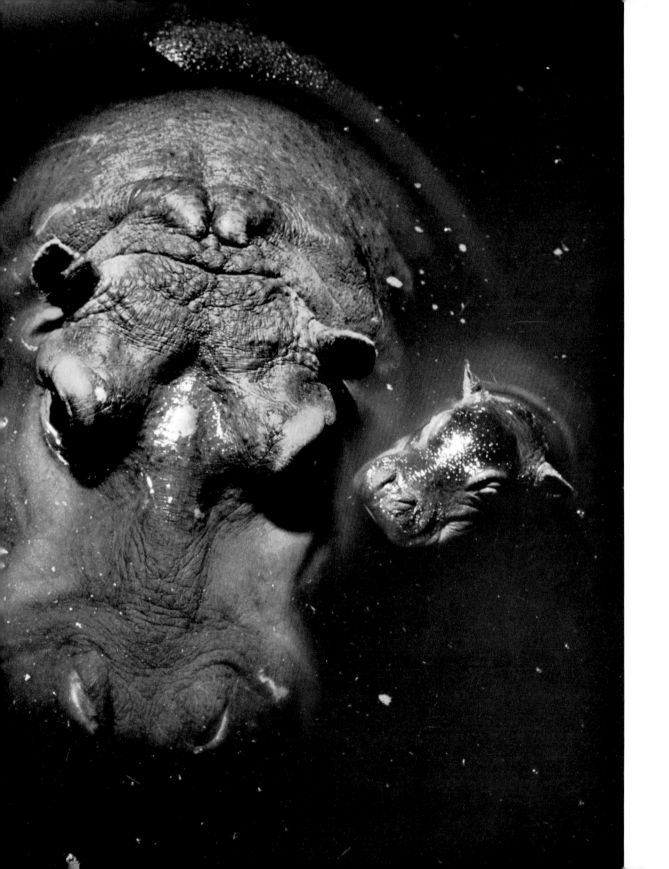

The baby hippopotamus which floats beside his mother has already had a big adventure. He was born underwater and rose to the surface for his first breath. Hippopotamuses are born swimmers. The babies are nursed underwater.

The seal calf was born on land and had to be taught how to swim. As soon as he can, he accompanies his mother far out into the sea.

The large
emperor
penguin
knows how
to adjust to
life on the ic
coast of the
South Pole.
To protect th
eggs from
the cold,
the penguin
parents kee
them bet-
ween their
legs and on
top of their
toes. The
penguin
parents take
turns doing
this till the
eggs are
hatched. Th
penguin
chicks also
warm them-
selves by
nestling in
their parents
toes.

Polar bears live in the northern polar regions. The cubs are born in a sheltering snow cave. The mother bear keeps a very close watch over her babies, watching over them also when they sleep. After they have grown their coat and can walk by themselves, they may leave the cave. When alarmed, they run back to their mother to take cover between her fore paws as this cub is doing in the picture.

Tortoises do not recognize their own babies. The tortoise mother lays her eggs in a hole she has dug which she covers up as soon as she is through. The eggs are hatched by the warmth of the sun. The mother need not look after the baby tortoises which are perfectly capable of looking after themselves.

The dromedary baby must learn early to move with the herd. Right after birth he is tied to his mother and follows her wherever she goes.

As though emerging from a sheltering rain roof, the ostrich chick pops up from his mother's feathers. Once the eggs are hatched, the ostrich parents lead their chicks away from the nest. When there is danger, the mother takes the babies away, while the father faces the enemy. When the weather becomes unbearably hot, the ostrich mother opens her wings to shelter her chicks.

An hour after being born, young zebras are on their legs to follow the wandering herd. With the herd, they are safe from the hungry lions or hyenas waiting for a weak or a sick zebra to feast on. The zebra mother and her child appear to be similarly striped, but that is not so. Among a thousand zebras, there are no two striped alike.

Baboons are very careful when they have their young. While carrying her babies, the mother baboon looks around slowly, in all directions, to see if there is any approaching danger. This way the baby clinging to her back learn to be careful also. Because the wandering herd i large, baboons must learn early to look after themselves. For a baby, the safes place to be is on his mother's bac

Spider monkeys are good climbers. They climb the trees of their South American habitat with great ease. The spider monkeys have 5 limbs: 2 arms, 2 legs, and a long tail, which is used as a third arm and can also be used like a hand. When climbing, they fasten themselves to the tree with their tail; it serves as a balancing pole when they run. The spider monkey baby is carried pick-a-back.

The habitat of the Abyssinian sacred baboon is more the rocky crags of the mountain where he sleeps than the plains where he spends most of the day. When wandering down to the valley or returning to the mountains, the herd remains together under the guidance of a chief, usually the strongest male of the tribe. Young baboons go off on their own earlier than most monkeys. However, they nurse longer than the others; going back to their mother from time to time to

suck a mouthful of milk is nothing new. Monkeys have a stronger maternal instinct than almost any other animal. A mother monkey never leaves her baby alone, but carries him wherever she goes. The gibbon baby, cuddled in his mother's arms, is carried everywhere. As soon as he is born, he will attach himself to his mother, clinging fast to her fur and not letting go.

The baby elephant weighs about 50 pounds at birth and is already over 3 feet high. Protectively the mother stands over her month old baby. When young elephants drink, they must roll up their trunks. Young elephants have thick hair covering their body.

The young African rhinoceros can follow his mother about a day after his birth. At two weeks he starts chewing grass.

Vicuñas are the most lovable member of the llama family. Vicuñas have the finest animal wool. For this reason they have been hunted ruthlessly in their Andean home Today there are not very many vicuñas left. The vicuña foal is jealously guarded by his mother, who becomes dangerous when one tries to pet her baby.

Lion cubs have a lightly colored fur coat with dark spots and stripes. They are born tiny, only half as big as a full grown house cat, and need long care before they can roam with the lioness. Lions are frequently reared in our zoos. Seeing a playing lion cub is an unforgettably beautiful experience.

Kangaroos are natives of Australia. They belong to the marsupial family (animals who care for their young in a pouch). Kangaroo babies are born tiny and under-developed. They creep into their mother's pouch to grow up. The babies grow a coat to cover their hairless skin. When they can see, they start peeking out of the pouch. They leave it only when they can hop after their parents. Sometimes they creep back into their mother's pouch even when they are old enough to have babies of their own.